MW00648625

CAT'S
MEOW

By Suzanne Beilenson

PETER PAUPER PRESS, INC.
WHITE PLAINS, NEW YORK

For Tom and Kitty Cat

Copyright © 1993
Peter Pauper Press, Inc.
202 Mamaroneck Avenue
White Plains, NY 10601
ISBN 0-88088-762-1
Printed in Singapore
7 6 5 4 3 2 1

INTRODUCTION

Why are we so utterly
fascinated by the feline?
Perhaps it's the cat's air
of mystery that holds us
so entranced, and makes
us want to learn more
about him.

We think that the trivia
and tidbits contained in

this little book will amuse and delight cat fanciers of all stripes. Just turn the page, and discover a few of the secrets our feline friends have been keeping quiet!

S.B.

CAT'S  MEOW

You can't keep a secret?
Always letting "the cat
out of the bag"? Don't
worry. You're not the
first. In the 1700's, scam
artists selling a "piglet"
would put a cat in the
bag instead. If a potential
buyer wanted to see the
pig, the con man would

CAT'S  MEOW

claim that it might escape
if he opened up the bag.
The cat often didn't like
being in the bag, however,
and if the swindler
wasn't careful, soon the
cat would be out of the
bag, his secret revealed,
and he would lose a sale!

CAT'S  MEOW

Among the winners of the PATSY award (Picture Animal Top Star of the Year) given out by the American Humane Association since 1951 are Audrey Hepburn's costar, Cat, from *Breakfast at Tiffany's*, and Morris from the Nine Lives Cat Food commercials.

CAT'S  MEOW

When an alley cat named
Charlie Chan inherited
an estate worth a quarter
of a million dollars from
his owner in 1978, it was
far from the first time
that a pet had received a
bequest. In the 1600's, a
famous harpist named

CAT'S  MEOW

Madame Dupuis left monies for the care and protection of her cats (along with very specific feeding instructions)! Her family, however, contested the will, and won the suit.

CAT'S  MEOW

Does your cat have
whiskers just to wake
you up when she climbs
into bed? Not at all! Cats
use their whiskers to
judge whether they can
fit into small spaces.

CAT'S  MEOW

Wearing a fur coat all the
time might account for a
cat's normal temperature
being about 102 degrees
Fahrenheit!

CAT'S  MEOW

With two young children
at home, John and Jackie
Kennedy naturally hosted
a number of pets while at
the White House,
including a canary, two
parakeets, scads of
hamsters, and three
ponies. Tom Kitten,
Caroline's pet cat,

CAT'S  MEOW

unfortunately had to be
relocated to the house of
Jackie's secretary. Why?
Because while Tom Kitten
loved to hang out with
the President, JFK's
response was purely
allergic. Gesundheit!

CAT'S MEOW

Ever wonder why a male cat is called Tom, and not Dick or Harry? Originally male cats were referred to as rams (Yup, just like sheep!). In the late eighteenth century, though, a popular story, *The Life and Adventures of a Cat*, featured a male cat named Tom. And Tom's been around ever since!

When Jimmy Carter took over the White House in 1977, his daughter Amy brought along her cat, a Siamese named Misty Malarky Ying Yang. A new puppy called Grits was soon after introduced into the presidential picture. The two pets, however, never hit it off, with Grits' main activity consisting of chasing MMYY.

CAT'S  MEOW

Who's the biggest cat of them all? Weighing as much as 650 pounds and measuring up to more than 13 feet including its tail, it's the Siberian Snow Tiger. Keep your distance if you meet up with this tiger. He could give Carl Lewis some competition in the long jump!

CAT'S  MEOW

One never knows when
one might run into the
dangerous Siberian tiger,
especially on a trip to
Asia. This big cat lives in
a wide variety of climates,
surviving the freezing
temperatures of Siberia
and also the drenching
heat of the Indian jungle.

CAT'S  MEOW

Every now and then a kingly sort of cat hob-knobs with the royal set. This certainly was the case with White Heather, a pet pussy of Queen Victoria of England. White Heather's address? Buckingham Palace, of course!

CAT'S  MEOW

If your cat turns up her
nose or makes a sour
puss when you offer her
a chocolate, it is because
cats are unable to taste
sweet foods.

CAT'S  MEOW

One of the reasons you
may find a dead mouse
or mole on your doorstep
at dawn is that a cat's
night vision is about six
times as acute as a
human's vision.

CAT'S  MEOW

A Texan tabby by the
name of Dusty gave birth
to more kittens in her
lifetime than any other
cat known. The grand
total? 420!

CAT'S  MEOW

There's good reason for calling the cat a hunter. Mickey, an English tabby, caught 22,000 mice in his lifetime, while Minnie, another English tabby, tracked down more than 12,000 rats in the six years she worked at the White City Stadium in London.

CAT'S  MEOW

Healthy cats can expect
to live about 15 years,
but you never know.
Puss, a British puss, born
in 1903, is said to have
lived to 36 years!

CAT'S  MEOW

The White House had
the honor of receiving
the first Siamese cat to be
imported into the United
States. In 1878, Miss
Pussy (later to be renamed
Siam by the stern Mrs.
Rutherford B. Hayes) was
sent as a gift by a
member of the U.S.
consulate in Siam. While

CAT'S  MEOW

greatly liked by the
Hayeses, Siam unfor-
tunately passed away
within a year of her
arrival. A Siamese cat did
not appear again at 1600
Pennsylvania Avenue
until Gerald Ford's
presidency a hundred
years later.

CAT'S  MEOW

The American cat population is estimated to be between twenty-five and sixty million. That's a lot of kitty litter, whew!

If while traveling abroad you happen to meet a foreign feline, it's helpful to know how to say cat in a few different countries: Gato (Spain), Koshka (Russia), Chat (France), Gatá (Greece), Katze (Germany), Neko (Japan), Chatul (Israel), Kot (Poland), Mao (China), Köttur (Iceland), and Kutjing (Indonesia).

CAT'S MEOW

Mark Twain, the famed creator of Tom Sawyer and Huckleberry Finn, was a feline *aficionado*. He gave his pet cats, though, obscure and difficult names such as Zoroaster and Blatherskite. He claimed it helped his children with pronunciation!

CAT'S  MEOW

As there is no breed known as a Cheshire, Lewis Carroll's inspiration for this grinning cat in *Alice's Adventures in Wonderland* is believed to have come from cheese molds shaped like cats— and produced in Cheshire, England!

CAT'S  MEOW

Who's the fastest cat of them all? The cheetah can clock approximately 70 mph over short distances. Domestic cats generally run at a little less than half the cheetah's rate.

CAT'S MEOW

The twentieth century has also spawned a new breed of felines—the Cartoon Cat! The first of these creatures was Krazy Kat, who appeared in the newspapers in 1910, and in silent film in 1916. Felix the Cat took over as reigning cartoon cat in the 1920's, and Tom (of

CAT'S MEOW

Tom and Jerry), and
Sylvester (who never did
catch Tweetie Pie),
Courageous Cat (and his
sidekick Minute Mouse),
and Heathcliff soon
followed. But the best-
selling cartoon cat of
them all has to be
Garfield, created by Jim
Davis in 1978.

CAT'S  MEOW

Presidential cat owners:
Abraham Lincoln, William
McKinley, Rutherford B.
Hayes, Teddy Roosevelt,
Woodrow Wilson, Calvin
Coolidge, Harry S. Tru-
man, John F. Kennedy,
Gerald Ford, Jimmy
Carter, and Bill Clinton.

CAT'S  MEOW

If your favorite feline
starts to purr, it usually
means she's having a fine
time. And if she rubs up
against you, she's telling
you that you're hers and
hers alone. But if the tip
of her tail starts to twitch,
look out for those claws!

CAT'S  MEOW

There are many legends
to explain why certain
cats, such as the Manx,
are tailless. The earliest
one, perhaps, relates that
two cats were late in
boarding Noah's Ark.
They slipped on just as
he was shutting the door,
but their tails were clipped
off in the process.

CAT'S  MEOW

The Cheshire Cat from *Alice's Adventures in Wonderland* is perhaps the most famous feline in literature. Though the book has never been out of print since its first publication in the 1860's (for years the Peter Pauper Press had a lovely edition), not everyone has always

been able to get a copy.
In 1931, the book was
censored in China for
some time because
animals spoke and were
treated as equal to
humans. Cats, no doubt,
would think they were
doing us humans a favor
by lowering themselves
to associate with us at all!

CAT'S  MEOW

The presidency of William
McKinley brought together
two important issues—
the Spanish-American
War and cats! When Mrs.
McKinley's angora cat
produced a litter of
kittens, she jokingly
named the two runts

CAT'S  MEOW

after the Spanish
ambassador and the
Cuban governor. The
joke turned sour, though,
when the war began
going badly for the U.S.
The two kittens were
sent off to be drowned.

CAT'S  MEOW

Americans are not the
only cat-loving culture.
French felines number
7,500,000, and the Brits'
kits are estimated at over
4,000,000!

CAT'S  MEOW

Cats may be solitary
creatures, but the wild
Iriomote cat takes the
cake. This rare type of
feline can be seen only
on a single island off
Japan's coast.

CAT'S  MEOW

One reason for the terrific speed cats have is that their entire foot doesn't hit the ground with each step. Rather, cats walk only on their toes and the balls of their feet. There's less friction— and more speed.

CAT'S  MEOW

One can find an indigenous cat on five of the seven continents: North America, South America, Europe, Asia, and Africa. Madagascar, a large island situated near the East African coast, interestingly enough, joins Australia and Antarctica in its lack of native felines!

CAT'S  MEOW

Everyone knows cats and dogs are mortal enemies, right? Perhaps not. Surveys indicate that one-third of all households that own dogs also have cats as pets!

CAT'S MEOW

Sir Winston Churchill
was devoted to his cats,
and he particularly favored
marmalade ones. How-
ever, of all the cats who
lived with him at 10
Downing Street (the
official Prime Minister's
residence), it was a Bob
(a black and white cat)
who ruled the front
steps!

CAT'S  MEOW

We humans may not always eat our vegetables, but the cat never does. Felines are strictly meat eaters, and judging by their personalities, they very likely would prefer filet mignon to hamburger every time!

CAT'S  MEOW

Even the gods love cats! The Roman goddess Artemis (known as Diana to the Greeks) was often depicted with a cat by her side. No wonder, as Artemis was also known as the Huntress!

CAT'S  MEOW

By the late 1980's, the
commercial cat food
industry's estimated worth
topped two billion dollars
per year, and eighty-nine
million dollars went to
kitty litter alone.

CAT'S  MEOW

The cat is one of the
most flexible characters
around, with the ability
to arch its back like a
horseshoe. This agility is
thanks to a spine and tail
made up of 44-58 verte-
brae (depending on the
breed). Human pet
owners, by comparison,
have at most 34 vertebrae.

CAT'S  MEOW

When the new king of
Siam (later renamed
Thailand), was crowned
in 1926, the processional
included a white cat,
which was said to carry
the previous king's soul.

CAT'S  MEOW

On average, a cat takes a
breath every 2.3 seconds
or 26 breaths per minute.

While pet owners vary
greatly in blood type,
their pet cats only come
in two varieties, A and B!

CAT'S  MEOW

The smallest cat of them
all is the Rusty Spotted
Cat, a wildcat found in
India and Ceylon. This
cat normally weighs in at
less than 3 pounds. Don't
try to bring one home,
however; they don't call
this cat wild for nothing!

CAT'S  MEOW

The cat has always been
a proud animal. It is
believed that the first
wild cats were domesti-
cated only 5,000 years
ago. Dogs, on the other
hand, were tamed
perhaps 45,000 years
earlier.

CAT'S  MEOW

Cat fanciers come in all
forms, and counted among
them are a number of
renowned writers: the
Brontë sisters, Mark
Twain, Ernest Heming-
way, Sir Walter Scott,
Charles Dickens, Henry
James, and William
Wordsworth.

CAT'S  MEOW

The largest litter ever
recorded was produced
by a British cat named
Tarawood Antigone. Her
19 kittens were delivered
in 1970 via caesarean
section. Of the fifteen
who survived, only one
was a girl!

CAT'S  MEOW

The Algonquin Hotel in
New York City may be
famed for the literary and
theatrical personalities
who have inhabited the
space, but two special
cats have been permanent
residents. Rusty made

CAT'S  MEOW

this hotel his home in the 1930's and 1940's, and was later succeeded by Hamlet. Out of love for Rusty, the hotel designated a special cat door to the kitchen for him—which Hamlet inherited.

CAT'S  MEOW

Sleeping an average of
16 hours a day, the cat
might seem a tad lazy.
However, the cat's physi-
cal make-up is designed
for quick bursts of high
energy. Therefore, the cat
is a great sprinter, but not
much of a long distance

CAT'S  MEOW

runner. With low en-
durance, the cat relies on
short periods of sleep
many times throughout
the day (Where did you
think "cat nap" came
from?) to keep in peak
condition.

CAT'S  MEOW

Ancient Romans just
adored their cats. The cat
was the only animal
permitted inside their
sacred temples. Arche-
ologists have even found
the remains of a cat
alongside its owner in
the excavations at
Pompeii.

CAT'S  MEOW

While everyone remembers the Cheshire Cat from *Alice's Adventures in Wonderland,* another feline appears in the story as well as in its sequel, *Through the Looking-Glass.* This literary kitty is Dinah, Alice's pet cat.

CAT'S  MEOW

Cat fancy has long been part of the Arab world. Muslims believe that Mohammed once cut off his sleeve rather than waken a beloved pet cat who was sleeping next to his arm.

CAT'S  MEOW

If you think that a black cat crossing your path means bad luck, be sure to avoid that great black cat, the panther. Of course, if it's the "pink panther," just give it some "rheume."

CAT'S  MEOW

Throughout the Middle Ages, black cats became associated with black magic and witches, and many were put to death. Some thought that they even contained the spirit of Satan. Later, black cats became in demand as household pets—to keep the devil away!

CAT'S  MEOW

Who says cats don't have heart? At 120 beats per minute, cats' hearts definitely exist!

The passenger list for the first dirigible to cross the Atlantic Ocean included Jazz, an adventurous tabby!

With their haughty demeanor, cats may think that no one has authority over them, but, in fact, cats are not above the law! Certain U.S. states have regulations on the books prohibiting cats from drinking beer, entering a fight between two dogs, and even pursuing ducks down a city thoroughfare.

CAT'S  MEOW

If you live in a tiny
apartment, a Singapura
cat is just the pet for you.
As the name implies, this
cat originally comes from
Singapore, and it is the
smallest domestic breed
around. Males weigh
about 6 pounds, and
females weigh only 4
pounds on average.

CAT'S  MEOW

The mid-1920's saw three
cats at the White House
home of Calvin Coolidge
and his family. While
Blackie and Bounder
appeared content with
the accommodations,
Tiger just never adjusted
to Washington. When he
ran away, the President

CAT'S  MEOW

broadcast a Missing Cat
Report over the radio,
and Tiger was soon
found and brought home.
The cat, however, was
persistent. Tiger ran
away again, and all efforts
to find him proved
fruitless.

CAT'S  MEOW

For more than a hundred years now, pet owners have been proudly displaying their cats. The first large cat show was held in London at the Crystal Palace in 1871, and cat shows have been popular affairs ever since.